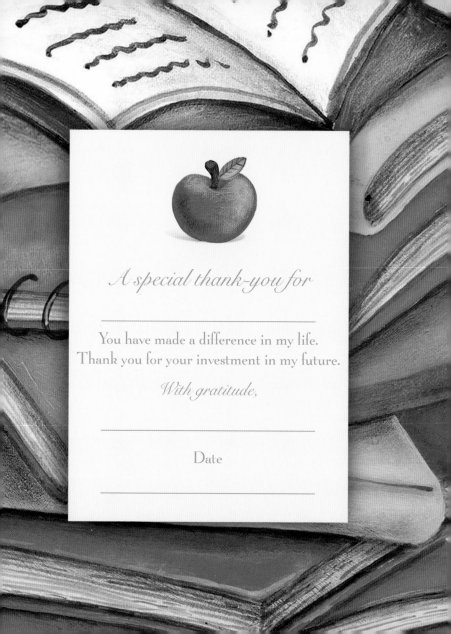

A special thank-you for

You have made a difference in my life.
Thank you for your investment in my future.

With gratitude,

Date

the
thank
you
s e r i e s™

Our purpose at Howard Publishing is to:

- *Increase faith* in the hearts of growing Christians
- *Inspire holiness* in the lives of believers
- *Instill hope* in the hearts of struggling people everywher

Because He's coming again!

Thank You Teacher © 2003 by Howard Publishing Company
All rights reserved. Printed in the United States of America

Published by Howard Publishing Co., Inc.
3117 North 7th Street, West Monroe, Louisiana 71291-2227

03 04 05 06 07 08 09 10 11 12   10 9 8 7 6 5 4 3 2 1

Stories by Caron Chandler Loveless
Edited by Between the Lines
Interior design by LinDee Loveland and Stephanie Denney

ISBN: 1-58229-309-0

thank you
you
teacher

a collection of poems,
prayers, stories, quotes, and
scriptures to say thank you

HOWARD
PUBLISHING CO.

thank you teacher

thank you teacher

thank you teacher

thank you

thank you teacher thank you teacher

thank you teacher thank you teacher

thank you

Your firm

support and

persistence have

enabled me

to accomplish

my goals.

thank **you**

teacher

Dear _____,

Each school day you faithfully challenge and plant hope in countless lives that rarely detect your sweet strategy.

You are a trailblazer. With you we trek the canyons of the mind, sail the seas of learning, and soar on flights of fancy.

You equip us with formulas, ideas, and practical knowledge that will endure. You stand as a provider of truth, determined that goodness, justice, and mercy will prevail.

Like an artist before her clay, you see the treasure hidden deep inside us. You are a master at calling it forth, giving it shape, and setting it free.

We may not always tell you, but we do notice your loving commitment—and we are grateful. Thank you for making a difference that will last a lifetime.

In appreciation,

thank
you

A teacher affects eternity; he can never tell where his influence stops.

HENRY ADAMS

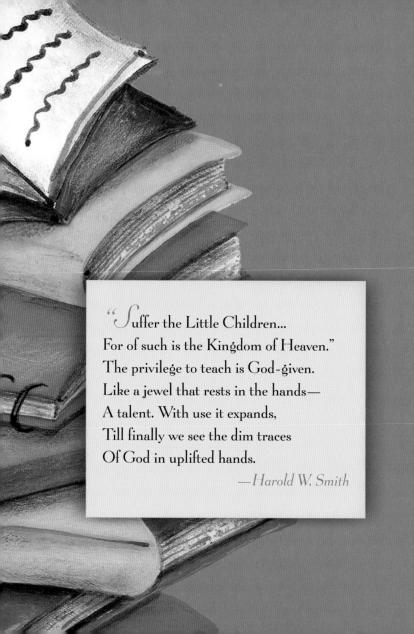

"Suffer the Little Children...
For of such is the Kingdom of Heaven."
The privilege to teach is God-given.
Like a jewel that rests in the hands—
A talent. With use it expands,
Till finally we see the dim traces
Of God in uplifted hands.

—Harold W. Smith

One Is All Right with Me

Cameras flashed, guests cheered, and music swelled as the groom wrapped the bride in his arms for a kiss. Then, bathed in a flood of warm candlelight, they strode down the flower-strewn aisle past Jean's row. The flushed, wide-eyed groom caught Jean's eye and winked. How dashing, how glowing and innocent this young couple looked, and how wonderfully curious were the circumstances that led Jean to join them this night.

It had been after school, just three weeks earlier. She was leaning over a desk helping a student with math when a sturdy young man walked in. At first Jean didn't recognize him.

"I doubt you remember me, Mrs. Maxwell," he said, "but I

was one of your fourth-grade students about fifteen years ago. I'm Dan Horton. It was Daniel back then."

"Well, let me look at you, Daniel," Jean said, scrutinizing him with interest. "Yes, Daniel! I remember you. It's so good to see you again. Has it really been fifteen years?"

"I'm afraid so," Dan said, pleased she'd remembered him.

"Well, look at you, all grown up and so handsome. A far cry from that scruffy little boy I remember. Let's see...weren't you...I seem to recall one or two incidents with you and another boy...what was his name?"

"Taylor. Taylor Vincent," Dan said, grinning sheepishly.

"You two were a couple of rascals. Didn't you pull the fire alarm once and hide out in the boys' room?"

"Yes ma'am. That was us."

"Well...Daniel," Jean chuckled. "How nice of you to stop by and see me. What brings you back to Emerson Elementary?"

"I'm getting married in a few weeks," Dan said nervously. "This may sound a bit strange," he continued, "but I was wondering if you would do me the honor of attending my wedding. It's here in town, so you wouldn't have to travel."

All Right with Me

"Getting married? That's wonderful! Who's the lucky girl?"

"Her name is Kelly-Grace Lockhart." Jean noticed Daniel's warmth when he spoke of his future bride. "We met in college. She's good for me. Keeps me in line."

"That must comfort your parents," Jean chuckled.

"Yes ma'am, it does," Dan grinned. "Listen, I know you've got work to do here," he said, reaching for an envelope in his jacket, "but here's an invitation. That's my penmanship on the front. As you can see, it's still pretty much the way you left it."

"Yes, I see that." Jean feigned disapproval.

"The wedding's in three weeks—on Saturday night. It would really mean a lot to me if you'd come."

"I'll see what I can do," Jean promised.

"Great!" Dan grinned and waved over his shoulder as he headed toward the door.

"Oh, and Daniel," Jean called after him.

"Yes ma'am?" Dan asked politely, stopping in the doorway.

"Let's have no pranks at the altar."

"No ma'am." Dan chuckled. Then he was gone.

In the twinkle-lighted reception hall, Jean found a place at the end of the receiving line and waited her turn.

One Is

"I'm Jean Maxwell, Daniel's fourth-grade teacher," Jean said, as a perky bridesmaid reached out her hand in greeting.

"Oh, Mrs. Maxwell! How great of you to come! Dan was so hoping you'd be here! I'm his sister, Shelly."

"Nice to meet you, Shelly. It was a lovely wedding."

"Wasn't it? Mrs. Maxwell, these are my parents. Mom and Dad, this is Mrs. Maxwell."

Dan's mother clasped Jean's hand warmly. "We're so honored that you came. You did so much for our son."

"Well, I'm glad to hear it, though I really don't guess I did anything special."

"We'll chat a bit later," Mrs. Horton promised, smiling. "I'd like you to know how important you've been to our son."

When the bride and groom's first dance was announced, Jean sat down at the nearest table. *What a dazzling bride,* Jean thought, as she watched the couple embrace. *Daniel has found quite a winner.*

After the dance Jean felt a tap on her shoulder.

"Mrs. Maxwell. I believe you're wanted down front." Dan's father stood beside her, offering his arm.

"I'm just fine here, Mr. Horton," she said. "Really."

All Right with Me

"This is Dan's idea," Mr. Horton said firmly. "He'd like you to sit with my wife and me."

"Oh, I couldn't," Jean protested.

"We insist."

"My goodness," Jean said, as she reached for her beaded purse and then stood and smoothed her dress. When she reached the family's table, Dan got up from his place beside his bride. All eyes followed as he walked toward Jean, cradling a bouquet of creamy-white Eskimo roses.

"These are for you, Mrs. Maxwell," Dan said with a broad smile.

"What in the world?" Jean asked with growing wonder.

"I know it's a little unorthodox," Dan said solemnly, "but it's my wedding, and I want to do this. I want you to know what you've meant to me."

"I'm speechless," croaked Jean, her throat tightening with emotion at the unexpected appreciation. "Thank you so much."

"Thank *you*, Mrs. Maxwell...for everything!" Dan said with feeling. "I'll never forget you."

"You're welcome, son," Jean said, tears glistening in her eyes. "For whatever it was," she added softly, as Dan returned to his bride.

One Is

"Mrs. Maxwell," Dan's mother said. "Please, sit down. It's obvious you have no idea what this is all about."

Jean shook her head. "Will somebody please tell me?"

"You were the only teacher who ever believed in Dan—who ever saw his heart and his potential," whispered Dan's mother. "Whenever he got in trouble—which we both know was often enough—you would tell him, 'Daniel Horton, you're a better man than this. You can't fool me. I see good things in you. What's the big idea of pretending to be some kind of hoodlum? Now go wash your hands, get to the head of that line, and march us out to the playground like the leader you were born to be.' Mrs. Maxwell, other than you, none of Dan's teachers had patience with him."

"I'm so sorry," Jean said, shaking her head again as Dan's mother continued.

"Year after year, his teachers either ignored or belittled him. One or two even mocked him in front of the class." The pain was still evident in Mrs. Horton's eyes. "We know he wasn't the easiest student to teach," she admitted. "But when Dan was about fourteen, he started saying things like, 'I'm so stupid. Everybody hates me. I don't blame them; I hate me too.' By the

All Right with Me

time he was sixteen, the situation had gotten so bad that he went to a nearby bridge, fully intending to jump."

Dan's mother's eyes glistened as she reached for Jean's hand. "And do you know what kept him from going through with it, Mrs. Maxwell?"

"My goodness, no. What?"

"You did," she announced, pausing to let Jean fully absorb the impact of her statement.

"What...?" Jean exclaimed, confused.

"Dan told us later that, as he prepared to kill himself, he remembered you and your faith in him. Somehow, he believed you'd be disappointed if he gave up. He couldn't bear the thought of disappointing the one person who really believed in him, so he didn't jump. So now, on the most important day in his life, Dan wanted to share it with the person who made the rest of his life possible."

Jean's mind raced in a million directions at once. *I can't believe this. Can it be true that I've played such an important role in this young man's life? How could anything I did ever make such a difference? What if I had failed to touch this boy's higher nature?*

One Is

How many other students are in desperate need of love and encouragement? Am I doing all I can for all the Daniels in my class this year?

"Thank you for telling me, Mrs. Horton," was all Jean could think to say aloud as she struggled to maintain her composure.

Driving home, Jean had to pull her Buick to the side of the road. She sat there for a long time. When she wasn't wiping her eyes and blowing her nose, she thought about her life, her teaching, and what she'd learned that evening.

When she got to school on Monday, Jean did exactly what she'd done every day for thirty years. She put her coffee on the side table, plopped some graded papers on her desk, and opened her lesson book. Then she folded her hands on the crease in the page and said aloud, "Father, help me make a difference in some child's life today. Just one is all right with me."

Next, Jean did a new thing. She took a single white Eskimo rose out of her bag and dropped the stem in the empty bud vase at the corner of her desk. Then she got up, sipped her coffee, and in perfect cursive penmanship, wrote the math assignment for the day on the chalkboard.

All Right with Me

thank you teacher

thank you teacher

thank you teacher

thank you

thank you teacher thank you teacher

thank you teacher

thank
you

Like the strength

from a needed

hug, your

investment in

my life

instills me with

confidence.

a blessing for you

$\mathcal{M}$ay you taste the joy of knowing

$\mathcal{Y}$our life has left a print

$\mathcal{O}$n the many hungry students

$\mathcal{W}$hom to you the Lord has sent.

teacher

May you smile as your investment

Accumulates each hour

And leaves a rich deposit

In the souls that you've empowered.

thank you teacher

thank you teacher

thank you teacher

thank you

thank you teacher thank you teacher thank you teacher

thank
you

As the sun

brings a bud to

blossom, so you

have opened my

eyes to truth.

Proverbs
6:23

NIV

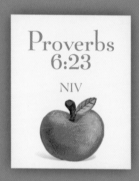

TEACHING
IS A LIGHT,
AND THE
CORRECTIONS
OF DISCIPLINE
ARE THE
WAY TO LIFE.

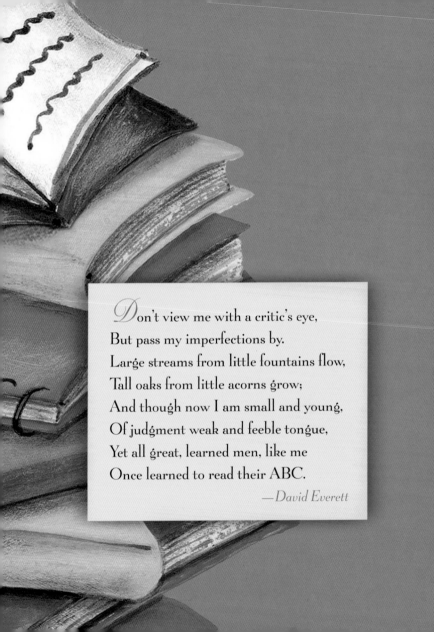

Don't view me with a critic's eye,
But pass my imperfections by.
Large streams from little fountains flow,
Tall oaks from little acorns grow;
And though now I am small and young,
Of judgment weak and feeble tongue,
Yet all great, learned men, like me
Once learned to read their ABC.

—David Everett

thank
you

The teacher is like the candle which lights others in consuming itself.

ITALIAN PROVERB

Just Like You

Brenda Carlson walked down the familiar hallways with her notebooks and lunch clutched to her chest in a posture of excitement mixed with fear. She surveyed the faces of a new generation of junior-highers talking and laughing. Subconsciously she was looking for someone she recognized, but the familiar halls were filled with strangers. Nothing had changed—yet everything had. Brenda felt as if she were in a time warp: It was ten years ago; she was thirteen again. It was a strange kind of thrill to think that she could share the world of these teens she would teach.

"Tim, forget your lunch?" a dark-skinned boy asked another. "Your mommy brought it for you," he taunted, nodding toward Brenda, instantly bursting her bubble.

It caused a similar reaction in Tim. "She's not my mother," he protested, blushing. "It's probably Becky's sister's parole officer."

This brought laughs from many students, but one tall, dark-haired girl slammed her locker door and stomped off down the hall. Brenda guessed it must be Becky. Empathy for the young girl almost overshadowed her own sudden feeling of being old. Almost.

Brenda was still pondering the scene when she reached room 282, opened the door, and saw the white-haired woman who would be her supervising teacher. "Oh good, you managed to find me," Ms. Madison said, glancing over her shoulder as she finished writing the day's math problems on the chalkboard. "Most student teachers have trouble navigating these winding halls their first time." She turned with a welcoming smile.

"But it's not my first time," Brenda said with a grin. "I was a student here ten years ago...in this very room. It was Mr. James's room then—"

Just then the bell rang, and students poured noisily into the classroom. Brenda recognized Tim and the dark-skinned boy from the hall—and there she was, the last one in: Becky. She looked as miserable and angry as she had in the hall. She sat in

Just Like You

the very back, slouched disinterestedly in her seat, and looked only at the door or the floor.

Brenda took the empty seat next to Becky, and one of the boys whispered loudly: "Hey, Tim was right—maybe she *is* here to keep an eye on 'Jailbait.'" There were muffled laughs as Ms. Madison called the class to order and introduced the new student teacher. Becky shot Brenda a pained look and sank even lower in her chair.

Brenda felt miserable. She had wanted to make a difference in someone's life, but not like this. On her first day, she had made this poor girl's life worse! Brenda breathed a quick but heartfelt prayer—that as Ms. Madison helped her to become a teacher in the coming months, she might help Becky in some way.

With ten minutes of class time left, Ms. Madison instructed the students to start on their homework. Students turned busily to the problems.

Becky just stared at the door.

"You're not working?" Brenda asked quietly.

Becky just shrugged.

"If you need help..." Brenda offered, but Becky cut her off savagely.

"I don't need help," she hissed. "I can add well enough to know my life doesn't add up to much. I've got a crummy family, and that's all anyone expects of me."

Brenda tried to hide her shock. She reached over, opened Becky's notebook, and wrote an equation across the page. "Think you know how it's going to come out, eh?" Brenda challenged. "No matter how many parts of the equation are already filled in, you can change the outcome radically by the values *you* plug in."

Becky seemed equally shocked at Brenda's response, but she studied Brenda's face. "You don't know what it's like," Becky muttered.

"I know what it was like for me," Brenda replied. "My parents had my life all planned out for me. They just assumed I'd take over the family business one day. They couldn't see that I wasn't like them." Her voice trembled at the memory.

"But ten years ago, a teacher encouraged me to follow my heart and discover what I loved most. Mr. James said that no one else could determine my life's course. Only I could choose. I chose to be a math teacher," she finished softly. "Just like him."

Just Like You

 *teacher*

"You have the power to change the equation of your life," Brenda said firmly, after a poignant pause. "Be what everyone expects you to be, be what other people are, or dare to be everything you *can* be."

As the weeks passed, Brenda learned bits and pieces of Becky's story. Before Becky was born, her father had been in prison for burglary. Becky's problems had escalated when her older half-sister was arrested for shoplifting—twice. Becky had become sullen, angry, and defensive at the cruel taunts of other students. Once an above-average student, Becky had lost interest in academics. Brenda resolved to do everything she could to make a difference for Becky.

"Ms. Carlson, you *are* coming to graduation?" Becky asked, as she slammed her locker door.

"I wouldn't miss it," Brenda answered.

"Great, because afterward, I have something to tell you." Becky smiled, then hurried away.

What a difference a few months makes, Brenda thought. Ten weeks ago she had been a nervous student teacher just praying to survive her first day, and Becky had been a sullen, at-risk kid who was down on herself and the world. They both had come a long way.

That evening, Brenda felt a sense of accomplishment and pride as each of "her students" stood to receive his or her diploma. Afterward, Becky came bounding up to greet her.

"Congratulations!" Brenda exclaimed.

"Thanks, Ms. Carlson," Becky said breathlessly. "For everything! You don't know what a difference you've made in my life."

"You're a smart girl, Becky," Brenda said earnestly. "Just believe in yourself. I do!"

"Thanks for being my friend, for making me do my math—and for trusting me when no one else did," Becky continued.

"Thank *you*," Brenda said. "That means a lot to me."

Becky grinned. "That's not all...I've decided what I want my life to add up to. I'm going to be a teacher, Ms. Carlson—just like you!"

"Just like me?" Brenda repeated, stunned but overjoyed. *Just like me*, she thought the words again. Yes, she really had become a teacher. She had made a difference.

Just Like You

thank you teacher

thank you teacher

thank you teacher

thank you

thank you teacher thank you teacher

thank you teacher thank you teacher

thank
you

Like a craftsman

with fine silver,

you polish my

potential and

help me to

shine.

Luke
6:40

NIV

A STUDENT
IS NOT ABOVE
HIS TEACHER,
BUT EVERYONE
WHO IS FULLY
TRAINED WILL
BE LIKE
HIS TEACHER.

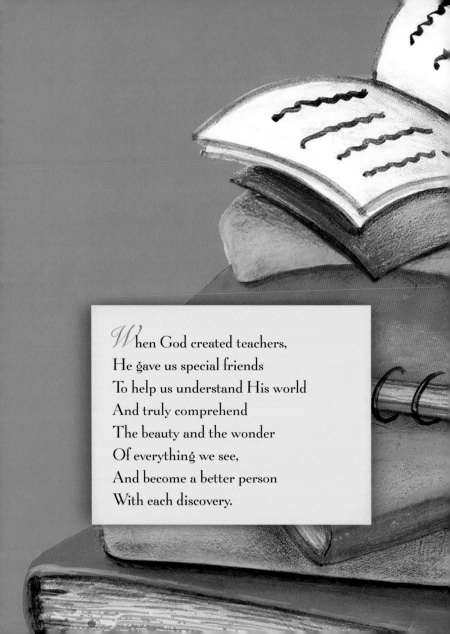

When God created teachers,
He gave us special friends
To help us understand His world
And truly comprehend
The beauty and the wonder
Of everything we see,
And become a better person
With each discovery.

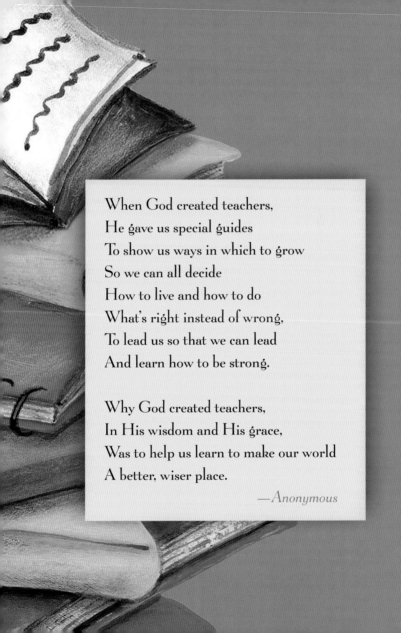

When God created teachers,
He gave us special guides
To show us ways in which to grow
So we can all decide
How to live and how to do
What's right instead of wrong,
To lead us so that we can lead
And learn how to be strong.

Why God created teachers,
In His wisdom and His grace,
Was to help us learn to make our world
A better, wiser place.

—*Anonymous*

thank you teacher

thank you teacher

thank you teacher

thank you

thank you teacher thank you teacher

thank you teacher thank you teacher

thank
you

Your words,

like a sturdy

foundation

beneath a high

tower, have

helped me to

stand tall.

thank
you

teacher

Dear Heavenly Father,

As You give out Your grace for this day, grant my dear teacher everything needed to carry out the great calling You have placed upon her. Bless her with peace as she walks the halls and wrestles with countless requirements and duties. Grant her love sufficient to fill the void she will see in someone's eyes. Give her wisdom in puzzling circumstances.

Great giver of all good gifts, pour out Your most precious blessings on this dear one so richly and abundantly that, as she faithfully leads others, she'll lack nothing for her own needs. Help her to know that her investments in the lives of her students have not been in vain.

But most of all, grant her unspeakable joy in the journey You've set before her. May she laugh with the heart of a child as she sees the fruit of her life's work blossoming in the next generation.

Amen.

School is a building that has four walls— with tomorrow inside.

LON WATTERS